# ONE MAN'S WEED IS
# ANOTHER MAN'S GRASS

**Roger Sweet**
**One Man's Weed Is Another Man's Grass**

All rights reserved
Copyright © 2023 by Roger Sweet

Published by BooxAI
ISBN: 978-965-578-813-6

# ONE MAN'S WEED IS ANOTHER MAN'S GRASS

SONG LYRICS, POEMS AND A SHORT STORY WRITTEN
BY A GUY WHO PLAYS WITH WORDS THE WAY
TODDLERS PLAY WITH FOOD

ROGER SWEET

# CONTENTS

# ACKNOWLEDGMENTS

This book is dedicated to my friend, lover, and wife, Gail, who, for 57 years, provided a steady sense of purpose, compassion, and tenacity to keep her quirky hubby from going too far off the rails.

To our kids Rob, Ann, and Ania (daughter-in-law). It is amazing to realize what each of you have contributed to the well-being of others through your medical careers. It is an honor and privilege to continue remaining a part of your lives.

To long-time buddies John Flaten, Steve Kluz, and Mike Rohr). who you can blame if you experience an unpleasant upper GI episode after reading all or part of this book. They are the guys who talked me into this book after reminding me I was a poet, not a musician, and that I should publish a book of poems and song lyrics. Thanx guys!

To John Austin, Joel Peskay, Steve Yussen and Skip Campbell longtime friends and professional colleagues with whom war stories and professional advice were shared. To Diana Bridgett, who gave me the initial jump start for completing this collection. To Bianca Reis who functioned as my Booxai program manager. She had to deal with a disorganized, book publishing rookie with limited computer skills. She was patient and supportive to the point where she should be considered a candidate for sainthood. Thanx to the following musical collaborators for providing their talent and critical advice: Chan Poling, Maurice Jaycox, Bob Ekstrand, Tom Krochock, Lars Nelson, Levi Rohr and Chris Granias

# AUTHORS NOTE

Hi there. I'm happy to see you've made it this far. I'm a retired psychologist living in Arizona, where one can idle away the hours engaging in a large variety of activities. So why did I also decide to devote a lot of time attempting to publish a collection of lyrics/poetry? The answer is a no-brainer. Vanity and legacy. On the vanity side, I would like to believe, or at least hope, that a few folks surmised that I produced something of critical and/or entertainment value. More importantly, before my expiration date, I wanted to create something tangible for family and friends.

Since the early 1990's I've been writing song lyrics and an occasional poem or short story. Some of those lyrics have been produced. However, I'm not a performing musician nor a music theory maven. I collaborated with professional musicians to develop melodies and arrangements. Along the way, I had 3 different pals (Steve, Mike, John) at three different times, living in three different towns, all telling me that I'm a poet, not a musician, and that I should publish a book of poetry/lyrics. Part of me still believes I'm a "songwriter", but they did have a point. Anyway, I went through over 140 "sort of finished products" and from that, winnowed it down to a collection that might be good enough for publication.

With exception of the title's commentary which comes first and one short story, which comes last, the poems and lyrics are presented alphabetically. In some cases, especially the produced songs, it's an obvious song lyric. With other items, it may be less obvious and yet, could be viewed as a potential lyric. Still, some of the items are clearly poems.

Due to copyright issues, if you're a musician or civilian planning to use any portion of this collection, including previously produced songs, contact me at 70sweet64@gmail.com.

# ONE MANS WEED IS ANOTHER MANS GRASS (COMMENTARY)

One man's weed is another man's grass. That's what I keep telling my neighbors and friends, who listen politely to my diatribes about the pain in the ass hassle of having the privilege of pushing a snarling, smoke spitting, upchucking, rock spewing beast over a weak excuse for an overindulged green plant that would never survive a long hot summer if not for the expensive gobs of synthetic sheep dip, cow shit, herbicides, insecticides and mega-gallons of H2O.

These comments are NOT directed at folks who truly enjoy taking care of their lawn. A close friend of mine fits into this category. If he sees one blade of crab grass it's "fire in the hole". I'm exaggerating a bit, but not by much.

My comments are directed at those of you who still carry a mortgage surrounded by a lawn. You would rather be doing just about anything other than maintaining your lawn and thinking about all the time and money it takes to keep it looking "acceptable" enough for your neighbors, many of whom feel exactly the way you do.

Remember the movie "THE GRADUATE" starring Dustin Hoffman? Hoffman's character has just graduated college and is being given advice regarding his career. The iconic word of advice was "PLASTICS". It jogs the person's memory about the film's content. I'd like to suggest the following iconic phrase as representing how to simplify the caretaking of your piece of earth. "CREEPING CHARLIE".

No, this is not a joke. Yeah, I know what you're thinking. He's a lunatic, another eco-weirdo. Everybody knows that Creeping Charlie is a noxious aggressive weed. I guess it's all in the eye of the beholder. You call it a weed. I call it natural GROUND COVER, which has been in use for hundreds of years.

There are a couple caveats to consider. It will strangle adjacent plant growth, so put some distance between Charlie and your favorite bushes or flowers. You will also have to keep it out of your neighbor's yard.

Advantages are numerous. It is tough as nails. It doesn't need to be watered every or every other day. Weekly works just fine. It can take a lot of punishment. No matter how often you neglect or abuse it i.e., lawn party for 300 of your closest friends, daily rugby, etc., it grows back aggressively. Much of the growth is horizontal, which means a lot less mowing. It has a nice post-mowed smell. In the spring, pretty violet flowers bloom, waiting to be pollinated by bees, birds and wind. There's a very long history of medicinal benefits. Oh, and don't forget. It could save you some dinero and a whole lot of time, while helping the environment. I'm done making my pitch. Think about it.

# ADORATION

Your eyes

those blue, sometimes mischievous eyes

that can see truths, even when tears cloud the sky


Your lips

soft lips I fondly kiss and nibble

lips that can communicate so very much

without uttering a single word


Your perseverance,

your hard nailed strength, your magical wisdom


I give myself

to your love and passion

# AIN'T MANY DAYS.

Born too restless, easily bored the teachers claimed

Every job I ever had always ended 'bout the same

Shooting off my mouth showing up late or not at all

Oppositional said the dude with the MD on his wall


Disappointment and frustration my oldest friends

More days than not I wish my life would end

You'll find me on a corner with a cardboard sign

I wave n' smile as you drive by while your eyes ignore mine


Desperation got no bounds nothing left to play

So into a Dallas bank, I walked to steal their money away

But just before I drew my gun this guy shakes my hand n' says

You're our ten millionth customer gonna make you a wealthy man

Ain't many days you get a second spin
Ain't many days a sin becomes a win
Rags to riches this was my lucky day
Better pinch myself before reality drifts away

Bank gave me a million bucks and a caddie deville,
Paid cash for a mansion up on blue berry hill
got women of every shape n' size sweet as sugar
Whatever I want they happily deliver

Bet you guessed by now I'm all shuck n' jive.
No money, car, no mansion, no women in my life
Oh I did rob a bank that ain't no lie
Just made it out the door as the cops arrived

Now to keep from going crazy i spend my time
Making up new lives better than mine
The prize I won in the end
Eighteen to twenty-five in the Huntsville state Penn

Ain't many days you get a second spin

Ain't many days a sin becomes a win

Reality bites my ass every day

Until the lights go out n' realty drifts away

# AS LONG AS YOU'RE NEXT TO ME

Fate drew us together

Roulette lovers aimlessly spinning around

A random event in the galaxy of love

Brought you to me

That first touch

Electricity turned to fire

What a crazy delight

Feeling alive

As long as you're next to me

As long as you're next to me

We played the game

Took our time read the signs

So much to learn

Young blood passion tamed by time


But then we touch

Electricity turns to fire

No need to rush

This long and deep desire

Love you so much my crazy delight

Feeling alive

As long as you're next to me

As long as you're next to me


There's no drug could get us any higher

Love you so much my crazy delight

Feeling alive

Whenever you're next to me

As long as you're next to me

# BINARY HERO

Binary hero

Pushing ones and zeroes

running before he hits the ground

spinning deals from Lexus wheels

Going round and round and round


Well-balanced family

Symmetrical harmony

Wife and one per gender

mood's always stable

Never swears at the table

Control he doesn't surrender


Pisses off no one

A likable showman

big white toothy smile

a real gift for the gab

For sure he'll pick up the tab

if you'll just stay with him awhile


Binary hero

Pushing ones and zeroes

running before he hits the ground

spinning deals from Lexus wheels

Going round and round and round


Sleep comes hard

Inside a house of cards

Steel doors shut down tight

Till dark rolls in

Arm n' arm with gin

N' stowaway dreams of the night


Cold rain biting, white hot lightning

High wire man in the middle

fear grips his face

As he falls into space

Couldn't grab on to the riddle

Darkness all but gone it's almost time to rise

High wire soon forgotten he opens up his eyes

Frozen in the mirror grinning ear to ear

Frozen in the mirror grinning ear to ear

Double talker, tightrope walker, success stalker

Binary hero

A one or a zero

spinning deals spinning wheels

Going round and round and round

# BLOOD UPON THE SHEETS

Deep in the blue ridge mountains, Josie Ann was born

Parents Earl n' Dora, brothers Jake n' Thorn

Blond hair, soft blue eyes said nothing of her fate

Became the family play thing long before she turned eight


Earl taught her lots of games, spare the rod spoil the rule

Dora taught her when to smile and denial of the truth

When Earl's friends came 'round, Josie closed her eyes and

traveled to her magic place, far away from secrets n' lies


**Dark shadows in her room THE DREAM haunts her sleep**

**Dirty hands, ugly sounds, sour breath on her neck, she silently weeps**

**Running through thistles a voice yelling you're mine to keep**

**Awakens to scratches on her arms and legs.**

**Blood upon the sheets**


Never missed a day of school but often wasn't there

Josie never said much, was labeled as impaired

Parents told the counselor she talks just fine at home

County closed the file, family cover was never blown


Years go by, just turned 16 never told a soul

But just beneath the surface, a volcano began to grow

Planning how and when to run away

But until that day family games still had to be played.


**Dark shadows in her room THE DREAM haunts her sleep**

**Dirty hands, ugly sounds, sour breath on her neck, she silently weeps**

**Running through thistles from a voice yelling you're mine to keep**

**Awakens to scratches on her arms and legs**

**Blood upon the sheets**


Josie's only companion her pet rabbit Ned

She loved him making sure all his needs were met

One day Josie begged Earl to please leave her alone

To punish her he grabbed Ned n' slit his throat down to the bone

Tears froze that day white rage burning in her throat
But still did as she was told obedient to a note
Climb on up here honey, I'm nice n' hard
Said yes sir as she climbed on top and stabbed Earl in the heart

Plan in place the EZ truck stop, free ride for a one-night stand
Just another runaway in the heart of a dangerous land
I'll ride you if you drive me, she'd learned her lessons well
What the future held in store was impossible to tell

Whatever happened to Josie no one really knows
Never did turn up as just another Jane Doe
But every year on the date of her daddy's demise
Some dude turns up with a hole where his heart used to reside

**Dark shadows in her room THE DREAM haunts her sleep**

**Dirty hands, ugly sounds, sour breath on her neck she silently weeps**

**Running through thistles from a voice yelling you're mine to keep**

**Awakens to scratches on her arms and legs.**

**Blood upon the sheets**

# BOTTLE OF JACK*

Lost my job n' my retirement pay

While the boss flies around in his private plane

Sent the good jobs overseas,

Made a ton of money now i'm history

**What's a man to do when the world turns black**

**Trade them blues for a bottle of jack**

Crib's under water, I'm 6 months behind

Banker man said boy, you're out of time

Sheriff came, took my house away

Latest squeeze booked the very next day

**What's a man to do when the world turns black**

**Trade them blues for a bottle of jack**

**Trade them blues for a bottle of jack**

**Warm glow flows from my head to my ass**

**Feeln' real tough ain't gonna take no crap**

**Trade them blues for a bottle of jack**

Repo man took my car

Now I'm traveln' light smokn' used cigars

Don't give a damn, don't think about much

Spend my days staying out of touch

**'cause I know what to do when the world turns black**

**Trade them blues for a bottle of jack**

**Trade them blues for a bottle of jack**

**Warm glow flows from my head to my ass**

**Feeln' real tough ain't gonna take no crap**

**Trade them blues for a bottle of jack**

Trade them blues oh yeah

Trade them blues oh yeah

Crap keeps com'n but I don't duck

Can't help myself I just stay drunk


Trade them blues for a bottle of jack


* Music/Arrangement by Maurice Jaycox and Bob Ekstrand

# CAT'S N' DOGS *

Cats n' dogs get along just fine so why can't you take the time

to love me,   oh baby just love me

If sweet n' sour can taste so good come on n' cook in my neigh-
borhood

some lovin'  sweet sweet lovin'.


So I didn't pay the bills on time  your birthday I'd forgotten

don't always drop the toilet seat and I drink straight from the carton


But if  cats n' dogs get along just fine  why can't you take the time

to love me,  oh baby just love me


I washed a dish we went to church watched the soaps together

mowed the lawn cleaned the john, hell I even called your sweet old mother


So if cats n' dogs get along just fine  why won't you let me try

to love you,  oh baby, to love you

hot n' cold turn to  steam  when we're  dancing  jean to jean

lovin,  sweet sweet lovin


So  when  this  old  bee  comes  buzzing  round,  you  don't  have  to  swat me

down

just love me  baby just love me


Sorry, I don't mean to stare  but your door was open wide

I've seen that funny look before a little twinkle in your eye

was that a nod to come on in,  goodbye silent night

say,  if  I  jingle  your  bells  just  right  won't  you  sleigh  my  guide  tonight


Cats n' dogs get along  just fine how about let's take the time

oh baby love me    oh baby   just love me   oh baby love me now


* Chan Poling: Music/Arrangement/Vocal

# CELEBRATION OF A GAY MARRIAGE

Love's journey kick started and fueled by passion and play

Maintained and enriched

Through sharing your minds and bodies

Surrounding a core of wisdom

Built upon countless years traveling arm n' arm along a road with an occasional straight away, but also many blind curves, potholes and road blocks where "they" scrutinized you

Before or if "they" were going to let you thru

While failing to warn you of bad weather ahead

Something happened on the way through time

"they" either smiled and waved or looked away

The road blocks were torn down

The fog burned into sunshine

In the bright light of the day

Let us celebrate as the final knot is tied,

Joining your already commingled souls

# COUCH POTATO BLUES

Watching life go by in my Lazy Boy lounger, at home inside my home.

The lawn and bills are way past due.

The wife thinks my mental status should be looked into.

I'm a certified couch potato sitting in a room with a view.


Not enough hours in a day to catch all that cable has on display.

Whose dirty laundry is on parade?

Trivia is a main pursuit. Game shows are really cool.

Reality TV, from jungle survival to Shark Tank Crew

The Soaps, those I sleep through.

PBS makes my head ache, listening to all those science flakes.

but I love my politics n' war. So much fun keeping score.

Can't ever get enough of that weather catastrophe stuff.

For sex, drugs n' crime it's HBO, Netflix n' Prime,

and the serial binging is so pleasantly addicting.

ESPN for sports of all shapes and sizes.

And the sitcoms are always full of predictable surprises

Demonstrations and court house barricades.

How many mass shootings How many graves


But being a couch potato is no free lunch.

Recently had my third heart attack. Told I better change my act.

Doc's orders, stop smoking or your will you better start composing.

Still, sneak extra smokes out back what's a little hack attack.

105 pounds north of normal, been told the problem ain't hormonal.

Blood pressure's 178 over 93.

Next time, hold the bacon on my double jumbo w/ cheese.

# DICK AND JANE

Flower child grew wild too fast

Daddy taught her all the facts

Jane taught herself not to feel


Lonely nights with lonely fools

Paid her tender loved her cruel

Trading tricks for tracks up her sleeve


Dick survived two desert wars

Now it's on and off detox wards

Chasing demons chasing him


Every dream's a horror show

Memories in his head explode

Killing other people's kin


Dick n' Jane side by side

Living under concrete skies

Broken glass n' railroad tracks

At the end of the line


Years beyond any second chance

Dick meets Jane in drug rehab

His sixth her fifth time thru


Booze n' meth hit it off just right

Grope therapy at first bite

Two heads worse than one


Revolving doors going round n' round

Twenty-one days and its outward bound

See Dick see Jane run


Found a place where they could crash

Under a bridge by the railroad tracks

Shared their bodies and their drugs of choice

Dick n' Jane riding high
Trippin n' lovn' under concrete skies
Broken glass n' railroad tracks
At the end of the line

Dick sold blood n' used his welfare check
Jane's body took care of the rest
Always feeding the beast that keeps them on the run

Lots of laughn' lots of lovn'
Lots of pushn' lots of shovn'
Lots of black n' blue to go around

Love fades fast when you got needs
Only booze n' needles can relieve
When aches n' shakes are never far away

Dick's too sick to sell his blood
Jane now weighs around eighty-one
The smell of death and desperation is in the air

Soon thereafter, Dick's liver quit

Jane's heart blew out after her last hit


Dick n' Jane lay side by side

Bagged n' tagged under concrete skies

Broken glass n' railroad tracks

At the end of the line

# DONT FORGET YOUR SENSES

When walking with your worries

Let the moonbeams dance along

Don't forget no, don't forget no

Don't forget your senses


When the heat ain't there and the rhythm's gone,

Your thoughts alone they won't make songs

Makes you oh so, oh this makes you

Oh so apprehensive

Don't forget no, don't forget no

Don't forget your senses.


Wave not your money in my face

Just cash in your pretenses

Go power trip another's space,

Hope it gets expensive

Money cannot save your face,

All worth the same in the graveyard place

Try to be yeah, try to be yeah,

Be yeah less offensive

Don't forget no,

Don't forget no don't forget your senses

When ones you love are in the storm

Don't forget your senses

A hurricane's eye is safe and warm

Got to feel protected

But safe with all that hell around,

Means senses could get run aground

Do protect them, don't forget them

Learn to keep your senses

Do protect them, don't neglect them

Hang on to your senses.

When with your love you've been too long

You need to mend some fences

When other love bait comes along,

You best collect your senses.

Or by the time you sneak back home,

You'll find yourself asleep alone

Don't forget no,

Don't forget no,

Don't forget your senses

# DREDEL SONG

I had a little driedle I made it out of **clay**

Spinning driedelat my friends house where we laugh and play

Oh driedel driedel driedel I maded it out of clay

Spinning driedel with my friends we laugh and play all day


I had a little driedle, I made it out of **wood**

It went spinning off the table and landed on my foot

Driedle dreidle dreildl I made it out of wood

It spun right off the table and landed on my foot


I had a little dreidel, I made it from a **rock**

When I finished spinning, I put it in my sock

I had a little dreidel, I made it from a rock

When I finished spinning I put it in my sock

When I spin my dreidel it skips and hips and hops

Until it gets all tired and then it finally flops

When I spin my dreidel it skips and hips and hops

Until it gets all tired and then it finally flops


I spun my little dreidel and much to my surprise

Spinning faster and faster and faster it flew into the sky

My spinning little dreidel much to my surprise

Spinning faster, faster, faster it flew into the sky


Then my spinning dreidel was grabbed off by a dog

He ran real fast and far away and hide it in a log

My yellow spinning dreidel was grabbed off by a dog

He ran so fast and far away and hide it in a log


Sitting on that log was aristocrat the cat

He grabbed the spinning dreidel and dropped it in my hat

Thank you thank you thank you aristocrat the cat

For dropping my yellow dreidel in my baseball cap


All day we play with dreidels we yell and shout and laugh

When we get all tired we stop and take a nap

All day we play with dreidels we scream and shout and laugh

When we get all tired we stop and take a nap


Went looking for my dreidel in my room, oh what a mess

Even turned my toy box upside down and much to my distress

My deidel it was broken i'll bet you'd never guess

My dreadel it got stepped on by Tyrannasouris Rex


When toys are spread all over in your messy room

That's when toys get stepped on or disappear from view

So keep your toys where they belong so you won't get upset

When you get a visit from tyrannasourosu rex


*Performed by yours truly at a nursery
school for 4 and 5 years olds.*

43

# DRIVE ME TO DRINK I'LL PAY FOR THE GAS*

I was a 12-step redneck dryer then a bag of dust

Blew off my old friends, hadn't touched a drop in months

But I sure could use a beer and a little touch

Couple of curves in the road couldn't be that dangerous


Skin tight jeans, black hair, eyes so blue

She had a Lone Star by the neck n' her scent what's a man to do

After a couple of dances, she whispered I know what you need

Jump off that wagon come on up n' ride with me


Silly putty in her hands I didn't stand a chance

Never gives credit, just takes cash

But she takes me places where there ain't no map

You drive me to drink baby, I'll pay for the gas

Since that fateful night, plus 7 years of regret

No longer blows kisses, throws dishes instead

Says don't wait up as she saunters out the door

Leaving me and Jack Daniels holding down the store


Silly putty in her hands I never stood a chance

Never gives credit, just takes my cash

But she takes me places where there ain't no map

You drive me to drink baby, I'll pay for the gas


She still digs places where the only free thing is air

Doin' 100 miles an hour she just wants her share

She's getting hers I'm getting mine

I'm at the bar and she's way over the line

But we both know who's driving who home tonight


Silly putty in her hands I never stood a chance

Never gives credit, just takes my cash

Still takes me places were where there ain't no map

Keep driving me to drink baby, I'll pay for the gas


*Chan Poling: Arrangement, Melody*

# FAST FOOD LOVE*

A torch and an empty bed was all you left

Good things don't always last she said

Still, imagine dirty dancing cheek to cheek

Still, hear us pillow talkn' in my sleep

How to live with you in my head

Fast food love to put my heat to bed


Love and money changing hands at the promised land

here's my new friend angel looking so grand

Same long black hair same sky-blue eyes

Same lavender scent makes me burn inside

How to live with you in my head

A look alike to put my heat to bed

Fast food love appetizers are free

Fast food love who you want me to be

Fast food love empty words for dessert

Fast food love's been served


We sing n' dance to the same old song. As my new friend angel plays along

Pretending it's you 'till the money's gone

Pretending it's you 'till the money's gone


Couple hundred cools the heat for a while

Y'all come back soon she smiles

Feeln' painless but empty 'bout as good as it gets

'Til you're back full time livn' in my head

Empty hits bottom i'm way down low

Feeln' lost but i know where to go ............ for more


Fast food love appetizers are free

Fast food love who you want me to be

Fast food love empty words for dessert

Fast food love has been served


Fast food love fast food love fast food love

Fast food love has been served

*Tom Krochock, Lars Nelson: Arrangement, Melody*

# GAIL VERSUS DANDELIONS

Sitting on the backyard deck trying to read but unable to get past page 1

distracted by Gail down in the yard among the Creeping Charlie

Weeding dandelions

But she doesn't just weed dandelions

She ATTACKS dandelions

On her knees

Digging, gouging them out of the ground

Oh, I almost forgot,

while simultaneously talking on the phone

Implement of destruction in her right hand and left hand on the ground

telephone nestled in the crock of her left shoulder

Attacks and talks

Gouges and talks

Pulls and talks

Stuffs and talks

Talks and talks


Dandelions never stood a chance

# I CAN HEAR YOU SINGING

It's midnight

Two gray tarnished candleholders

Sitting side by side on a squeaky-clean kitchen counter

Candles still burning white but they are beginning to dim

One in a pool of melting wax

Flickers on

The other has nothing left

And burns out

I can hear you singing


In a place where medicine goes about its business of salvaging protoplasm

In a room where the sun is outshined by digital displays

Going beep beep in the night

I can hear you singing


A petite fuzzy gray-hair

Glasses half on half off

Mouth half open half closed

Half sitting half lying

Holds on tight to the puffy perforated hand of her 60-year lover

Her other hand massages his protruding belly

Baby baby please pee for me

Probably not

But would you settle for a song


Passover Seder

Where the main attraction is lots of wine

Followed by the overdone, over the top, over-embellished

Key lay no yeh key lay no yeh

Boy!

Can I ever hear you singing


An old man with a dusty vacant look in his eyes, barely hanging
onto life So damn tired

But giving in to a son's request to sing at his granddaughter's
wedding

Thanks dad. I can hear you singing

It's 4 AM

When the loneliest of metaphors whistles by in the night while a son contemplates

Pencil on the left

Tears on the right

Drift away but not quiet into the night

I still can hear you singing

Someday let's do a duet

# I GOT LOU (PARODY OF "I GOT YOU BABE" BY SONNY AND CHAR)

I punched her so she hit me

with an OFP and a nasty divorce decree.

I don't like to work, don't follow rules

I'm an alcoholic and manic depressive too


Better hire Lou babe

So I got Lou, babe

Don't wanna get screwed hey

So I got Lou hey


Knew I had to cover my butt

Big time loser if I don't play rough

You're in good hands he puffed at me

Mud wrestling is the only way to be

I got Lou Babe

Yeah I got Lou babe

Don't wanna get screwed hey

So I got Lou hey


Really dug the way he pouts n' shouts

still got my pockets turned inside out

Loved the way he filleted that shrink

But lost the case n' I'm drowning in red ink


Thanx a lot hey

Between you n' her babe

I got screwed hey

lots of luck getting paid hey

# IF YOU WANT TO SUCCEED

I get away with lots of stuff,

Easy pickings, but it's never enough

Bible in my hand, wrapped around the flag

Libs say like a crazy man


Yeah, the elite and academics think I'm crazy, but that's alright

They scratch their pointy heads 'cause I keep 'em guessing day and night.


My faithful subjects believe every lie and empty slogan

For I am the ultimate showman

I make up lots of stuff these yokels eat it up.

Tough guy is what they respect and love

Screaming for blood so that's what I give 'em

Us against them they gonna take away your freedom

Fear, repetition, ignorance, and superstition

The perfect mix for the coming revolution

Stand back stand by

Make America Great Again our battle cry


The people who work for me must pledge undying loyalty.

Yes men and young hotties only need to apply

But fuck with me just once and it's under the bus

Plus political suicide


Kiss my ass or kiss my ring either way's ok with me

As long as it's done on bended knee

You're part of my brothel, the GOP


I call the shots you carry them out but,

If you get busted keep your mouth shut

Take the heat for me take a little jail time

When the heat cools,

I'll pardon your fake news crime.

Or put another way, as my whore

If things head south you will fall on your sword

Now El Duce' ruled with an iron hand

Too bad he ended hanging upside down like a slab of ham

He had looked so cool in his uniform and ribbons

Standing there over his minions.

Chin raised, chest out, hands on hips

Haughty frown, tight lips

I look just like El Duce' I'm so fucking virile

No one has to know I'm wearing a girdle


Almost made it on January sixth if it hadn't been for that chicken shit.

Pence, a guy with no balls or common sense

Don't need him anymore got my loyal lieutenants on the congress floor.

Stay tuned for 2024


So if you want to succeed follow me

The all-time master of grift n' greed.

# INTENSITY

My quiet thunder

Oh those rare so precious moments

When i feel the nuclear intensity of your soul

As it first surprises…

Then humbles…

And finally surrounds and enters me


My guard went on a well deserved permanent vacation

# INTERRUPTIONS

It's one clock in the morning

When the northern side of life finally makes its long overdue opening appearance

Through just opened windows too long locked tight

Against the silent blazing haze of jungle summer

Lying heavy and wet on top of wheezing asthmatic air conditioners

Which now lay silent

While in a Victorian living room open wide to changing winds

I sink into my favorite blue Buddha chair and close my eyes

Floating inside cricket rhythms chirp chirp chirp

While neighbors in driveways and streets

Laughing and chatting underneath street lamps and trees

Making shadows……………..

Deep inside the black oak woods

The campfire catches shadows of wind and trees singing a duet

And dancing the tango around the circle of Druids in white robes

Holding hands, swaying, murmuring chants

Drawing me into their circle from behind the trees

Where I was hiding


Home at last...........................just as the red eye special drones in from the west.

Shit!!!

# JUST ANOTHER DAY

Who are you who am I? Many decades side by side.

Went to the circus had a great time

First prize in the Richard Dreyfuss look-alike contest

Won the lottery

Knighted by the Queen of England

Got the big defense contract

Won a grammy

But without your love ……. It's all just another day.

# LET ME IN

That hopeful look in your eyes hoping I'll comply

Back to fakn' what you love to hear

You get what you need then you're fast asleep

And I'm lying here stuck in third gear


Used to trade our private thoughts lying side by side

Usually ended with lots of heat and a long slow ride

I'd get off like a rocket on the fourth of July

But for many moons, my tank's been running dry

It doesn't take a rocket science to figure out why


Sex by the numbers is now history

I'm done faking ecstasy

If we're gonna stay lovers

We got new ground to cover

Need to open your head n' let me in


Still good at slinging bullshit n' your gifts are really nice

Still, perform all the right moves, but darlin you've lost the spice

You hold too much inside your head for which we both pay a price

Gonna take hearing more about where you're at to melt this block of ice


Sex by the numbers is now history

No more faking ecstasy

If we're gonna stay lovers

We got new ground to cover

Need to open your head n' let me in


Need more action from the head sitting on your neck

That part sometimes seems sealed in cement

So listen up, 'cause here's what you need to know

For what it takes to curl my toes.

Didn't your daddy ever tell you

"son, two heads working together

Always works better than one"

So honey, open up your head n' let me in

# LIE WITH ME

Lie with me when desire has taken a vacation

Lie with me when your skin is hot but your heart is cold

Lie with me when you're feeling restless and lonely

Lie with me when fatigue overtakes reason

Lie with me when emotions are trapped in cement overshoes

Lie with me when demons are running drag races in your head

Lie with me so I can wrap my arms around your doubts and fears

Lie with me and feel the winds of change blowing in the window

Lie with me and we'll ride the winds of change together

Lie with me so I can watch moonlight dance around your body

Lie with me so I can whisper…

I love you

# MONDAY'S HEAT TUESDAY'S BURN

She was a quiet child, a picture of grace.

Early years spent in a dangerous place

But somehow she survived the games of secrets, lies, and denial

By learning to hide herself behind a serene smile.


But because of her history, she ignored some basic truths

About getting the hots for jealous, possessive fools.

The story was always the same at first blush.

He made her feel special, wanted, and loved.

What a rush!

**Monday's Heat Tuesday's Burn**


The honeymoon was short lived,

Ending when he knew she was his.

Everything stayed cool by telling him what he needed to hear.

But when he got drunk he got a lot more possessive and insecure.

Benign comments misperceived.

Pledges of loyalty and love not believed.

The lion roars and the fists start to fly.

She dries her tears, blots her cut lip, and ices her black eye.

The next day it's an apology, promises, and a pretty bouquet.

Back to feeling special, wanted, and loved.

Queen for a day.

**Monday's Heat Tuesday's Burn**


But this wasn't the first time nor was it the last.

Always hoped she could help him change.

But alas.

The only change was an ambulance ride, 3 cracked ribs, a busted jaw

And intervention by the law.

Yet it was a neighbor who took it upon herself to make the call.

**Monday's Heat Tuesday's Burn**


The fool got sentenced. Did 90 days plus probation.

Court ordered anger management, alcohol rehabilitation and a No Contact citation.

Our fool was no fool. He glided through

Anger management and alcohol treatment school.

Driven by possessive temptation.

He calls her, which was prohibited under the terms of his probation.

But in a New York minute, his words dissolve her resolve in the face of his pleading protestations.

She bought his rap believing he was on the reformed track.

Say goodbye to the order of No Contact.

**Monday's Heat Tuesday's Burn**

It was de ja vu like their first meet.

The only thing left was for history to repeat.

For one last time, the fool fooled her again.

No more denials, too late to pretend.

A love story, a lethal end.

**Monday's Heat Tuesday's Burn**

# MTG

I'm Marjorie Taylor Green, the neo-Aryan queen.

You watched me score on the congress floor.

ME and my new bud Kevin.

I stuck to him like glue, big toothy smile for the TV crews.

Every vote we held our ground, kept tightening the screws,

ME, n' the 20-patriot wrecking crew.

We played chicken better than the country club RINO center.

In the end Kevin, we granted you the little tin crown.

Better hold it on tight, because it's gonna get hammered by the ultra-right


Kev, you're gonna do lots of step n' fetch it, shuck n' jive

To keep your sorry ass alive. Because Kev,

I've got you by the you know whats,

You power hungry, feckless putz.


Just kidding Kev. Many thanx for Homeland Security.

ME and the wrecking crew with feelings of patriotic purity

Will ensure America becomes the bastion of white supremacy.


Oh also by the way, thanx for Oversight,

Giving ME and the wrecking crew the right with patriotic delight,

To cut n' slash left wing corruption,

And investigate, charge, and impeach those responsible

For the socialist disruption.


Assigned to Oversight only after being told I had matured.

I now rest assured, giving you the real details n' facts

So you understand that what I say n' think

Is exactly how I will act.


I'll admit being called a publicity hound, but hey

Good, bad or ugly makes no difference to me

Because the media gives me publicity for free, yes indeed.

But don't believe what they say, ——— ——— even if it might be true.

King Donald would still be number one if I'd been in charge of mob rule.

Would have sounded the alarm to come fully armed.

We could have served up an evangelical revolutionary stew.


Russia is our friend King Donald proclaims. Couldn't agree more.

Go ahead Vlad, nuke the Uks. Let 'em fry.

With King Donald back in charge, we'll send you a brief wrist slapping diplomatic reply.


Conspiracies are in the eye of the beholder. We behold and will be bold. Our enemies will not replace us! Our all-mighty God will bless us. Jews, coloreds, Muslims, gays, and all other less thans will be shown their place and station as we again become a white Christian nation.

We will undo all the stolen elections. No time wasted on reflection.


Gerrymandering and self -righteous intimidation are why my people believe I am a savior of our nation. I just might wind up alongside King Donald, at his 2025 inauguration.

# MY BLUES BE GONE*

I chose booze over you that was the final scene

Ever since that night, I have the same old dream

My ex-wife laying in my arms

She whispers one last time can't do no harm


Dreams don't last forever its 3 AM

Tossing n' turning can't get to sleep again

Then I start thinking how it could have been

If for all those years I'd loved her more than I loved gin


How long how long does this pain go on

How long how long 'for my blues be gone


It's been two years since that final scene

She got the house n' my kids but I got my dream

Eight hours at the factory home alone again

hot dogs n' beans, a 6 pack, catch the news at ten

Then it's time to catch the rerun playing in my head

So I'm never alone in my ice-cold bed

How long how long does this pain go on

How long how long 'for my blues be gone

How long how long how long does this pain go on

How long how long 'for my blues be gone

MY BLUES BE GONE

MY BLUES BE GONE

MY BLUES BE GONE

* *Maurice Jacox, Bob Eckstrand: Arrangement. Melody*

# NOW IS MY MOTHER

Now is my mother

Bent over in pain.

Skibbling across the kitchen floor

On 80-year-old legs.

Hot rolls just out of the oven

"eat another, you're too thin"


Then was my mother not so long ago.

Still in pain but jumping up n' down.

A Richard Simons Silver Fox.

Jump step… jump step… jump step


Then was my mother many seasons ago

Umpire baiter

Fog horn voice

"Open your eyes ump"


HAPPY 80th MA!!

# OMEN OF THE TREE :(A NOTE OF MELANCHOLY AND CELEBRATION)

ROB: Who I hope doesn't forget the scalpel in a personal injury lawyer's chest cavity.

ANN: Who finds that making a running, diving backhanded catch is a lot easier than sitting still.

As you both reach another "moving on" point, I wanted to write you guys a note, congratulating you and wishing you luck, etc. but instead wound up writing a something that conveys deeper feelings about moving on. Please accept this in the spirit in which it was written, as one who loves you both very much.

A believer in omens I'll always be

Ever since I saw the TREE

Outback kicking back, living in my head thinking…

A message for Rob and Ann

Rob

Four years ago a cardinal (UW Madison) flying from the Apple to the Oak

ANN

Four years ago "Fire and Ice"

Showing the world she was no joke


Omens of what will be.

The kids are leaving.

Time to let emotions run free


Gazing to the west, and oh!

There it was staring down at me

The treehouse oak, lifeless as can be

Its bare outstretched branches bonding sky and earth

I felt like the omen for the moment was that the dead tree was me!


Hey…but that's the way it's always been

Just look at all the life surrounding that dead tree

rough, disordered as such, and more than just a little green

Now that's an omen I can live with!


So if there's advice in there somewhere

It goes something like this….


As you go n' grow near or far

Always remember…

Omens are omens

That's for you to decide

But breaks are what you make

There's no free ride


Up, down, or sideways life is where you take it

Omens going round and round

I have no doubts

You'll make it.


In the end, life's a circle

Today you're the random pinball on a roulette wheel

Tomorrow the hands on a watch

The next day somewhere in between


My love to you both as we all continue our journeys

# ONE LAST PIECE OF FUDGE

I see you're still cruising around the speed of sound

In the monetary fast track on a global merry go round

But in those rare twilight moments 'tween reality and dreams

In those twilight moments when ambivalence reigns supreme

Where sometimes it doesn't seem enough sometimes it's way too much

Doesn't really matter if it's friendship, love, or lust

Could be the only answer is all of the above

It would be nice to share with you…

One last piece of fudge

# PROMISED LAND

Sunday morning do a little blow,

getn' high, going no place real slow.

Doorbell rings Jehovah's at my door.

This here pamphlet will show you the way to the Lord.


Thanks for your concern Mr. Blue Suit, but I know where I stand

Got my own directions to the Promised Land,

Where I be makn' moves to catch some dreams,

Score some touch, run a scheme.

Mojo workn' found both last night

A hoochie mama and a hot pair of dice.


Sunday noon, there's this Dude on the tube calling me friend.

Diamond rings on his fingers, promising everlasting life if money I send.

But those on the know, that after the show, when the lights go out,

he got his 14-year-old "friend" to make him twist n' shout.

If he ever gets caught with his pants around his knees, he will cry out, "the Devil took control, pray for me please."

The Devil my ass preacher man! Your sins are in your dirty little hands.

Difference 'tween you n' me is I know who I am and where I stand.

Where bull shit, lust, n' money flow like sand.

Down at the Promised Land.

# PROMISES*

Abraham my father where art thou

What happened to the promises you made

You promised to keep us safe teaching love instead of hate

Abraham my father where art thou


Isaac studies Talmud and sings the Shema

Ishmael learns Hadith and the Seven Laws

Ishmael prays to eastern skies

Isaac praying at sunrise

Adonai or Allah which art thou


Isaac calls his Sarah back in Tel Aviv

Against the wall leans his M16

Making plans for their wedding day

Making love from miles away

Milk and honey all around them


Ishmael dreams of Ashti lying in his arms

An AK 47 by his side

Humming a desert wedding song

Making love 'til the moon was gone

Starlight dancing all around them


Sarah and baby Moshe were blown apart

Ashti and baby Amud shot to bits

Two lovers no longer care

Their bloodlust wails fill the air

Vengeance, hate, and fear surround them


On the Temple Mount where trees of peace stand

Just before they meet hand to hand

Mortar shells hit the ground

Protoplasm all around

Cries of mother oh mother where out thou

Abraham my father where art thou

What happened to the promises you made

You promised to keep us safe teaching love instead of hate

Abraham my father where art thou


Blinded Ishmael pulls out his last grenade

Crippled Isaac pulls out his gun

Ishmael sets to pull the pin

Cold blue steel against his chin

Arab and Jew nowhere to run to


They grab each other's lethal hand

One crippled the other cannot see

Milliseconds to decide

Brothers for life or suicide

Tough life better than no life at all


Ishmael strums the Dotar standing in the dark

Isaac bangs the Tof he cannot feel

breaking through dogma walls to play their song in burning halls

singing

Abraham my father where art thou

What happened to the promises you made

You promised to keep us safe teaching love instead of hate

Abraham my father where art thou

*Chris Granias: Melody, Arrangment*

# QUIET THUNDER

There are times when watching you from a distance

I become consumed by my attraction for you but say not a word

Your soft graying hair, high cheekbones, soft white skin, blue eyes

Slender, long boned fingers surrounded by rings of white gold and turquoise born

From an earlier time. Beauty surrounding beauty.

Understated, classic beauty, a Kathryn Hepburn kind of beauty

But also a deeply sensual passionate beauty surrounded by an opaque wall

Until the smallest of life's simple pleasures make you smile, make you laugh, make

You sigh.

When I brush aside your hair and like a little child, you hum

When I touch your face and you gaze at me, eyes half open with a Cheshire cat

Smile

When I hold your face and look in your eyes where passion quietly waits.

Forever, my quiet thunder

# RAINING IN SEATTLE *

I found the chocolates hidden under the bed

Bittersweet kisses hard to forget


When it's raining in Seattle

The sun shines in my room

Wine is on the table waiting for you


You say all the right words you've got a plan

Meanwhile, it's love games whenever we can


When it's raining in Seattle

The sun shines in my room

Wine is on the table waiting for you

Lying here beside you your heart pounds in my head

When in a dream you sigh,

Her name instead


That far-off look in your eyes you'll be leaving soon

Bitter sweets and little white lies left behind in my room


Raining in Seattle

The sun shines in my room

Wine is on the table waiting for you


*Chan Poling: Arrangement*

# REBOUND LOVIN*

Got divorced six months before

Still feeling my way around the grocery store

Football sunday you'll find more

Football widows by the score


A friendly look in the coffee aisle

What do i do it's been a while

She's buying beans, i'm an instant guy

Should've known then to wink a quick goodbye

Should've known then to wink a quick goodbye


Grab your partner and come on down

Doe se doe love's on the rebound

Alimony left alimony right

This old heart's on the rebound tonight

She just made forty just made single
Just another restless midlife swindle
The so-called love of her so-so life
Traded her in for a trophy wife

She didn't trust men i was scared of women
Talk about going against your religion
Bet you didn't think i'd bounce back so fast
Rebound lovin i'm alive at last
Rebound lovin i'm alive at last

Grab your partner and come on down
Doe se doe love's on the rebound
Alimony left alimony right
This old boy's on the rebound tonight

Lost control with just a sigh
Lost ourselves and closed our eyes
Opened our eyes politely indifferent
Looks like another short-term commitment
Why did i think it would be any different

Grab your partner and come on down

Doe se doe love's on the rebound

Alimony left alimony right

This old heart's on the rebound tonight


*Chan Poling: Arrangement, Melody*

# SAFE HARBOR HOOK UP

Knocking around had one of those downtime moments

Caught in the dark, shot in the heart didn't even know it

Twisting and turning in my alibis

Get that little itch and I realize

Win or lose, you play you never outgrow it


You got the look of a long-lost love gone by

So do I

Bet you got taken for a real slow ride

So have I

Let's lose this loneliness

I remember our first caress

And the tiny heart around your neck

But the rain didn't last too long

Sun came out you were gone


This time did you find what you were looking for

Well neither did I babe

Don't wanna hear 'bout your latest shipwrecks

Sure as hell ain't gonna mention mine


Still wearing your tiny heart, please don't leave

I believe you need to stay here inside with me

Cause as far as the eye can see

There's a cat 5 on the horizon

# SEPTEMBER SIDE OF AUGUST*

Smokey melon sunset, mother nature's getting laid
Misty haze carries me back to careless yesterdays
Summer buns are humming, you're faking hard to get
September side of August, one last summer sweat

Searching for that lovn' feeling, fat man found his thrill
Sleepwalking under dashboard lights climbing our own hills
Young blood, gonna do run run, gonna have some fun tonight
September side of August, end of sum sum summer time

Young love flying high n' fast some crash some fly away
Some just forget to smell the rose they planted yesterday

Walked a lot of crooked paths got lost a few times too

Yesterday's in the rear-view mirror, but I'm right here next to you

I'm your sunrise baby, make you warm gonna make you shine

Yeah, it's September side of August, guess what's on my mind

Put your hands in mine

Still got some hills to climb

We'll take a real real long time

*Chan Poling: Arrangement/Melody*

# SOME WOUNDS NEVER HEAL

Spawned behind a backwoods dive

Born but failed to thrive

The family pet always forced to kneel

Learned how not to feel

Some wounds never heal


Their blood was upon his hands

Burned down the house by voice command

Learned to love but mostly learned to steal

When they wouldn't yield

Some wounds never heal


The lamb is taken by the fox

For a while, the voices stop

Flashbacks put back in the box

Which remains unlocked


The lamb and the fox

The nightmares never stop

They try to conceal

Scars that never seal

Some wounds never heal

Some wounds never heal

Some wounds never heal

# SUCK IT UP (GEEZER'S LAMENT)

Grandpa, what irrelevant literary contribution to society did you make during the Covid19 lockdown? Well son, it went like this…..

Suck it up suck it up

Geezer hood is rough

Beats dying most the time get down drink some wine

Suck it up suck it up


Mirror mirror on the wall

My boobs in freefall

Pants up to my pits love handles doing flips

Should I laugh or bawl


Belly fat to lose

Can't see or touch my shoes

Pipes all but gone not feeln' very strong

Down to five foot two


Suck it up suck it up

Geezer hood is rough

Beats dying most the time get down drink some wine

Suck it up suck it up


I get the posture talk

'bout the way I walk

Lopsided gait can't you stand up straight

Hey man, it's not my fault


My hearing kind of sucks

Why folks yell at me so much

Can't see well at night do I turn left or right

Forget which end is up


Peed too often day n' night

Got my prostate sliced

Cum don't come out any more whole lot neater than before

Still kept my appetite

Suck it up suck it up

Geezer hood is rough

Beats dying most the time ......get down n' drink a shit load of wine

Suck it up suck it up


Cha Cha Cha

# THE MESSENGER*

In the woods my friends and I, commando games all-day

Make believe in no man's land, shoot to kill for play, until

The day my dad cried goodbye and left an empty space

Now the battlefield's a fast -food lot between two camps of hate


Two houses without a home, they divvied up the rest

Couldn't keep me out of it, they tried their very best

Tell her to get you here on time, tell him his check is late

Couldn't tell each other nothing except behind each other's face


There goes the messenger across the empty space

There goes the messenger passwords all in place

There goes the messenger frozen smile upon his face

Don't shoot the messenger don't shoot the messenger

Weekdays living with my mom go to school breaking rules
Weekends listening to my dad, always singing the blues
Loving and hating them at the same time
How did I contribute to their crime

The firing stops as I step out on to the open plain
I carry tired old words of hurt between two worlds of pain

There goes the messenger across the empty space
There goes the messenger pass words all in place
There goes the messenger frozen smile upon his face
Don't shoot the messenger don't shoot the messenger

My son Johnny waves a smile at me and runs off on his own
Off to fight battles with his friends or fight all alone
I watch her as he hops and skips out toward the enemy
Slumped inside our four-wheel tanks, repeating history

There goes the messenger across the empty space
There goes the messenger pass words all in place

There goes the messenger frozen smile upon his face

Don't shoot the messenger don't shoot the messenger

*Chan Poling: Arrangement, Melody*

# THE ROSE*

Many years together slowly digging ruts

Taken things for granted not talking very much

Ruts getting deeper

Foundation getting weaker

Hassles over total crap

You annoy me i annoy you back


'til it's war, fighting for survival

Then it's make-up sex, jungle love style

Warm fuzzies last a day or two

'til the same old same old takes its due

Another rose dries up n' drifts away


Let's plant a new rose tonight never let it drift away

Let's eat some humble pie, leave some time to play

When we're, feeling lost sweet memories find a way

To keep the love light glowing even on rainy days


Shouldn't have to fight before playing in the jungle

Shouldn't have to fight before feeln' loved n' humbled

Shouldn't have to fight before tasting bitter/sweet fruit

Shouldn't have to fight before saying I love you


Let's plant a new rose tonight never let it drift away

Let's eat some humble pie, leave some time to play

When we're feeling lost, sweet memories find a way

To keep the love light glowing even on rainy days


Come wrap your legs around my waist

N' your soul around my heart

Let's plant a new rose tonight


*Levi Rohr: Arrangement. Melody (Rough Draft)*

# UNTITLED

Number 60 ain't that far away

Glad we decided that it's ok

To do what it takes

To stop little mistakes

From making "I love you" harder to say

Because…..

I love you when the sun shines

I love you when it rains

Even when your back is turned

I love you just the same

# UPSTAIRS DOWNSTAIRS

I'm down stairs chasing youth while the grim reaper's chasing me

She's upstairs pondering a 30 across, 8-letter word meaning, "to accept life more graciously"


I'm outside walking the dog and talking to myself

She's inside stroking the cat and talking on the phone


**I'm inside watering the plants**

She's outside killing dandelions


I like watching the "Terminator"

She watches the "Antique Road Show"


I collect thoughts and hoard nuts n' bolts

She collects jewelry and hoards paper wrap

I'm just trying to plan my next 5 minutes

She's already planned our funerals

I can lie down and not have a thought in my head

She lays down thinking about what she's thinking about

I'm still trying to keep up with Peter Pan

Her childhood ended at 16 when her Peter Pan died and

broke her heart

# WHATEVER

I know what I need

I know what you need


You know what you need

You know what I need


There never is

Nor will ever be


Whatever

# WINTER RITUAL

It's early spring, and winter is having respiratory problems

But that old cold bastard can still kick some ass

When your pain center least expects it.


But it's 5AM where even at the nighttime low

The juices are running.

You can see it in the street

You can smell it in the air

mid-march just the other side of Ides

When it's time to make war

Upon the output of man's best friend

It is time for the early Spring turd patrol

It is time to get out there to seek and destroy

Hammer and pickaxe in hand

The ultimate disposal weapon

Pick up the hard ones on top of the hard snow

Chop n' roll out the icers

Dig out the ones buried in the snow banks

That still think it's winter

# YOU AND I

We will always see ourselves within each other's eyes

Reflecting light that keeps our feelings warm

Against the awful chill of useless storms

Until lightning ignites weary hearts

Stirring you and I to gaze upon each other's eyes

Reassured our love remains as real and clear

As the stars that witnessed our first kiss

# YOU ME N' US

Saturday we got nothing to do

How about you n' me hang in this afternoon


Play some board games maybe other games later

Listening to Saturday night blues lying together


No bicker no muss no fuss

Need some down time you, me n' us

# THE ROCK (SHORT STORY)

This story is about a boy named Willis, who everyone except his parents and other adults, called him "Wheel Eyes" because of his round, thick glasses. We'll just call him Will for short. One late summer day, Will was walking through the Lagoon woods on his way to his favorite secret fishing hole, that only he and 30 additional 10, 11, and 12 year olds knew about. Cold weather had come earlier than usual to Minnesota. Even though it was still mid to late August, a cool 5mph west northwest wind made it feel like the middle of September, when the woods release its crisp damp organic smell that one associates with the coming of Autumn.

Just as he was about to wade through a shallow creek, he almost tripped over something sticking out of the ground along the creek's edge. He squatted down to look at what had almost tripped him up. Partially embedded in the mud was this most unusual rock. It was oval and shaped like an egg. But where an egg's surface is smooth, the rock's surface was very coarse and rough, like #80 grit sandpaper. But the thing that really drew his attention were the sparkling colors caught by the sun's rays coming through the trees. He dug it out of the mud and rinsed it off in the creek. After wiping it dry, he held it up to the sunlight and was blown away watching this sparkling rock creating a constantly changing kaleidoscope of colors. Will also noticed the rock gradually became warmer the longer he held on to it.

Will had never been all that interested in rocks. Oh, on occasion he would find some big flat ones for water skipping. His record was 8 skips, which he managed to do once when there was no wind and the water was flat and sheer as glass. Sometimes on his way home from school, he would come across a round rock which he would try and kick all the way home without it veering into the grass. During the winter he would put stones inside snowballs to use against the junior high kids who would bug him and his friends on the way home from school. But this rock was different, special. Never before had Will come across a rock that sparkled, changed colors, or give off such an intense heat. He couldn't wait to show this rock to his friends.

He didn't catch any fish. He didn't even get a bite, but it really didn't matter. He ran home and hid the rock in his room. He wanted to keep the rock on his dresser where he could look at and handle it whenever he wanted. But he knew his parents would never let him keep a dirty old useless rock in the house. Also, If they knew it gave off an intense heat, they would really have a cow, worrying it might start a fire. Fortunately, he had the perfect hiding place for his rock. In the back corner of his closet where he always stashed his baseball gear, was a piece of wood that covered a square hole. He had no idea why the hole was there and couldn't have cared less. In his secret place were things his parents would surely get mad about if they ever found them. Inside an old wooden cigar box were two cigars he had stolen from uncle Jack's house last thanksgiving. He and Nick had tried smoking one of the cigars but ended up hurling after they each inhaled a couple of times. There was a rusty switchblade knife that only sprang out halfway that he found outside the rear entrance of the Majestic Movie Theater, where he and his friends would sometimes sneak in for free. There was a pack of playing cards of almost naked women his friend Nick had traded him in exchange for 6 tiger eye boulders. There was also a letter from Joleen, a girl he knew at school, who liked him, though he saw no reason to like her back, but he had kept her letter anyway.

He couldn't wait until tomorrow morning when he could show off his prize to his friends at East Moreland Park, where they gathered to play football. Most of the night he held the rock in his hands using a flashlight under the covers, watching the changing colors.

Early the next morning he took off on his bike without eating any of the pancakes his mother had made for him. He was the first to arrive at the park but didn't mind showing up early. He was just happy to wander around the park staring at his rock. Another half hour went by before other kids began rolling in on their bikes. Pat who was usually the first to arrive, asked Will why he had arrived so early. You see, Will never got anywhere on time, much less early. At first, Will had decided to wait until everyone had arrived before showing his rock. But he couldn't wait because Pat always was first to show up at anything or being first in line like at the school cafeteria and was real cocky about it. When Will showed Pat the rock, Pat got kind of a "what's the big deal" look on his face. Things quickly changed when he watched the sparkling rock explode into many changing colors in the sunlight while becoming hotter the longer he held it.

As the rest of the kids started showing up, they were wondering why everyone was hanging around the sideline bench instead of kicking or passing the football around. It wasn't long before everyone who got the chance to see and hold the rock wanted to know where he found it and if he wanted to trade for it. Nick was willing to trade back the 6 tiger eyes plus an additional 3 steelies. Dale wanted it so bad that he was willing to give up his baseball, which had been personally autographed by Warren Spahn. Tony, whose parents were rich, offered to pay him 5 dollars. On it went. Will almost traded with Nick. Boy, he really wanted those steelies, but in the end, nothing could compare with this strange, beautiful rock.

It's funny how a rock could make such a difference, for on that day when the kids were chosen to pair off into teams, Will was chosen first instead of near last which was usually the case. He wound up making lots of tackles. On a kickoff return, he made it to the other team's 15-yard line. He also caught a long pass in the end zone for the winning touchdown.

Things continued to go his way for the next couple of years. Other things also changed. Seventh grade was looming on the horizon. He also had to start preparing for his Bar Mitzvah. This meant attending Hebrew School every Tuesday and Thursday after school, which he hated doing. He became more interested in Joleen. He even took her to see the first 3D movie "Bwana Devil", which required wearing special glasses. It was really cool. He got to put his arm around her when she gasped as the lion appeared to leap out from the screen. At night there were other distractions, like this radio station transmitting from Little Rock Arkansas, which played a kind of music he'd never heard before. He had to wait until after 10 for the signal to come through clear enough. He would listen almost every night until 2 in the morning. Of course getting up for school became a major pain.

During the increasingly rare occasions when taking his rock out of the closet, he started to notice that while it still changed different colors, it did so less often. The colors also were less sparkling or bright. Also, it didn't feel as warm as before. Will continued to wonder why his rock was changing. However, he didn't wonder for long, and at some point during seventh grade, the rock had long since escaped into the world of forgotten things.

The story ends there. Well, sort of. Will finished high school generally in one piece and went on traveling down conventional paths ..... army, college, marriage, job, kids, mortgage, friends, etc., busy busy busy. When Will's life wasn't so busy, he was often overcome by feelings of restlessness and boredom... or even worse, nothing. It was always a bit disconcerting to feel nothing. Will made sure his life continued to be filled with many somethings.

However, there was one time of year when Will found not being busy to be a time of tranquility. During early Fall when warm southern winds slowly begin their northern turnaround and the bright blue sky becomes filled with groups of huge cotton ball clouds. That time of year when mother nature begins to paint her own kaleidoscope of colors among the trees. A time of year when Will experienced feelings of melancholy and excitement as he enjoyed the slightly sweet, organic, acidic odor of damp, decaying vegetation. His golden retriever Fletcher, also loved this time of year. So much to smell, so much to roll in. His favorites were dead anything and cow manure.

During one of these walks, Will became aware of a bloated sensation in his gut that transferred to his chest and head. At first, he thought he was having a heart attack. However, as the sensation quickly passed, he became misty-eyed as he recalled a long-forgotten memory of walking through his favorite woods in the town where he lived as a kid. The lagoon woods, the creek, his favorite fishing spot..... the rock.

He sat down on a tree stump and tearfully nodded his head and smiled as he thought back to that late summer day so many years ago when he found the rock with all the sparkling colors that kept changing the more you held it up to the sunlight... and the heat. The longer you held the rock, the hotter it became. He couldn't even remember the last time he had seen, much less held the rock. He reminisced about the day after his find, when he showed this unusual rock to his friends before playing football, and what a great game he played that day. "I wonder whatever happened to that damn rock", he said to himself. He assumed his mother probably found the box and threw it out, sometime after he left home after being drafted.

About a year after Will's emotional recollection of finding the rock, his folks sold their home and moved into Grandma's house when she was no longer able to independently take care of herself. Within a year, she died at the age of 92, having outlived three husbands. By then Will and his wife had been together for 13 years and had 2 children. Five years later, his mom died after a long bout with pancreatic cancer. His father died almost a year later after suffering his third heart attack. It was now left up to Will, who was an only child, to sell his grandma's old house. Before putting the house on the market, Will had to go through the house and figure out what to donate, what to sell, and what to throw away.

His grandmother's wood frame house was built in the 1920's. It was three stories, including a partially finished attic. As a kid, he had been in this house numerous times. His favorite place, of course, was in the attic. Will had always enjoyed searching through old things in out of the way or isolated places, which were no longer part of the mainstream of life. Will hadn't been in grandma's attic since he was maybe 9 or 10. It was the first place he went to look for items to be donated, sold, or thrown away. As he opened the attic door, the first thing he smelled was the dank combination of old wood, dust, mothballs and mold. Once inside, he had to clear his way through the spider webs, while keeping an eye out for bats.

He was meandering his way around some clothes and cardboard boxes when he looked down at what appeared to be an old cigar box. As he bent down to pick it up, thinking this couldn't possibly be the cigar box he had long ago hidden in the wall panel behind his closet. Son of a bitch! That's exactly what it was!

After finding an old wooden crate to sit on and blowing off the thick accumulation of dust, Will opened the box. Along with Nick's dirty picture cards, was the switchblade that only opened part way, Uncle Jack's 2 cigars (one of which was partially smoked- the one he and Nick got sick on), Joleen's letter (they wound up dating on, and off through high school) and there it was … his magical rock. He quietly said, "thanks ma" for not throwing away the cigar box and its contents.

Will picked up the rock and held it in the shaft of sunlight coming through the attic window. At first, it looked likely any other colored rock, but in a matter of a few seconds, it began to sparkle as if it were a huge diamond. Then it began to continuously change colors like the Northern Lights, except with more colors and different shades of color. Finally, his rock became just short of being too hot to handle.

Will still couldn't remember the last time he had held his rock. He thought he was maybe 12 or 13, but really wasn't sure. He vaguely remembered how the rock didn't sparkle so brightly and how the colors no longer were as rich or as varied or how the rock no longer generated much heat. However, he clearly recalled that early fall day a few years ago while walking through woods with his dog, when he experienced this epiphany triggered by the organic smells associated with autumn and remembered the circumstances surrounding how and where he found this strange rock along a creek bed.

As a curious 12-year -old, there was no way Will could have ever figured out why the rock seemed to change. However 40 plus years later as Will sat cross-legged on the dusty attic floor, he realized it wasn't the rock that changed.

At that moment a growing feeling of contentment swept over him. After a moment or two, he slowly got up with the cigar box, its contents in one hand and the rock in the other, and climbed down from the attic. Decisions about what to keep, what to sell, and what to toss would have to wait. He had more important business to take care of.

As he drove home, a short poem popped into his head. Much like the epiphany experienced a few years ago, the words led to a wry smile and misty eyes.


*Don't hide your rock in the box shut behind the closet door*

*You'll forget you ever had it you'll forget what it was for*

*Full of heat and color as long as you are there*

*Turns gray and cold not on its own, but because you didn't care*


*So keep it in the open, keep it in the light*

*Though far away you sometimes be, always keep it in your sight*

*Don't forget to hold it, colors need to be renewed*

*So easy to forget, that a rock has feelings too*

Made in the USA
Middletown, DE
24 August 2024